So, What's Your Excuse?

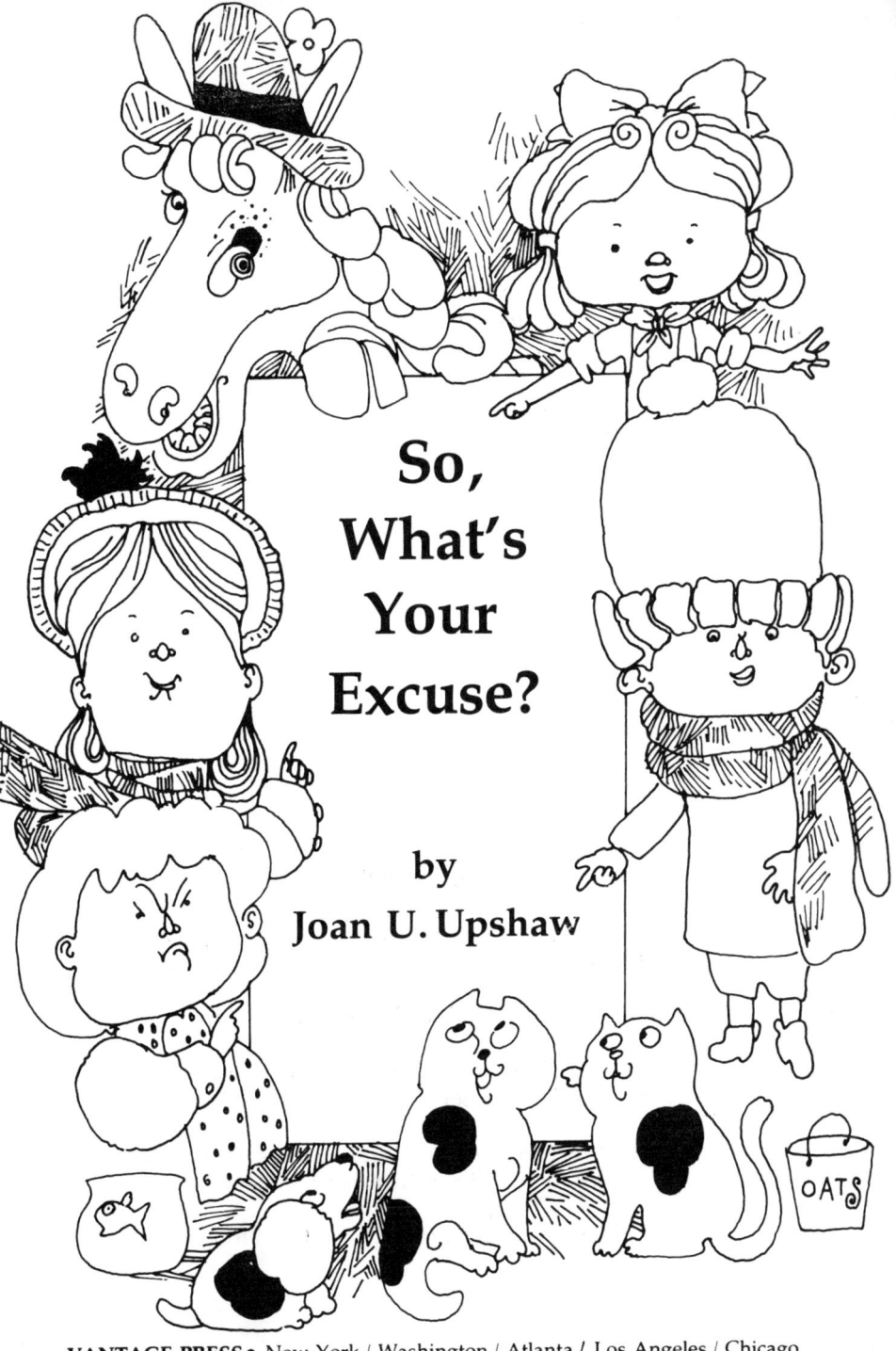

Illustrated by Warren Harlan

FIRST EDITION

All rights reserved, including the right of
reproduction in whole or in part in any form

Copyright © 1979 by Joan U. Upshaw

Published by Vantage Press, Inc.
516 West 34th Street, New York, New York 10001

Manufactured in the United States of America
Standard Book Number 533-04060-4

Library of Congress Card No.: 78-65172

Dedicated to

Norma F. Goalder,

an outstanding teacher
with a
grand sense of humor

FOREWORD

The following pages contain actual excuses written by parents for their children. Most of them explain why a child was absent from school; some explain other unusual circumstances. Names have been changed, but the grammar and spelling remain intact. These notes were collected over a period of five years from several school districts. They were selected for purposes of humor, but they also contain meaningful messages to those engaged in the field of education.

Joan U. Upshaw
Newport News, Virginia
January, 1979

So, What's Your Excuse?

DEAR TEACHER . . .

Please excuse Eddie from school due to his having a cold and some fever. He was also kicked in his side by a horse this week-end.
                            Thank you,
                          Mrs. Anderson

This is why Lloyd can't come to school yesterday, because I was sick with my head.
                            Thank you
                            Mrs. Brown

Kim has been sick with the flu. She still has a cold and sore throat, but she wanted to come to school.
                       Thank You,
                       Mrs. Cooke

Lisa had to go to a foot Doctor, she has flat foot, she has to be footed, I took her thursday, because she couldn't walk stright, I have to take her back tuesday, she has too wear it to she become a teen ager, if not longer, please excuse her, I hope the kids don't tease her.

                Mrs. Daniels

Tammy hase a very bade coild. i don't know why it is hanging on. She hase this coild for 3 or 4 weeks.

              Mr. Evans

Wanda was sick with here back. She have truble walking at times.

                Sign,
               Mrs. Fritz

Melissa was feeling sick at her stomack yesterday, and she may still feel sick at her stomack today, at times.

             Mrs. Gordon

Susie was absent Friday because she had a bad diareha.
                                          Mrs. Hill

        Jimmy was out of school yesterday, because his mother was having a baby. It was a girl. All are fine.
                                      Mr. Ingram

Please excuse Karen for being absent. The reasons are very personal. Thank you very much.
                                      Mrs. Jones

        Harriet was unable to attend school Thurs. and Fri. because she had poison ivory all over her face and her eyes are swell.
                                      Ms. Kennedy

Harry was out due to cold and cold sores around his nose. Happy New Year to you.
                                  Thank you,
                                Mrs. Lawson

        Jimmy had an ear ace yesterday. This is the reason I kept him out of school. His ear is still running but maybe he can make it today. If it is hurting you have my permission to give him an aspirin. I don't have anyway to come and get him.
                                  Thank you,
                                Mrs. Martin
P.S. Please let him stay in at recess, so he won't be getting air in his ears.

Monica was absent because I wash, and all of the clothes froze up.
                                Thank You
                                Mrs. Neal

        Cathy was absent last year because she has been sick.
                                  Fondly,
                                  Mrs. Owens

Please excuse Sally's absence from school last week—She had "the flu," and was truly a sick girl. No temp. past three days. I hope she will be O.K. in school. *Please* do not let anyone breathe, sneeze, cough or look in her direction. One more sick child and I will run away from home.

Yours in good health,
Mrs. Parker

Johnny was sick yesterday and he have headache at time, he hit his head to the seat on Firday.

Mrs. Queen

Joseph was absent because he had to see a skin doctor about his face. I know you had a nice day yesterday without you no who. (smile) Have a nice day.

Mrs. Robinson

Please excuse Patricia for the follow days that she miss school, 29th until now. She had physician injuries with her ankle.
        Mrs. Smith

    Please excuse Diana for missing Mon. and Tue. She had a ashama attack that kept her up and feeling bad. She still can't run but she's better if she sits still.
         Mrs. Taylor

Please excuse Mable from school yesterday as her father came home. She was so excited that she didn't sleep well and was real tired.
        Mrs. Ukrop

    Melinda was sick from the neddles we got at the health clince.
         Thank you,
         Mrs. Vest

Here I am again. I kept him home again, even though he did really want to go to school. Isn't that strange? For a boy who gets marginal grades, he sure is anxious to get to school. Anyway, here is another nice little excuse. I really wish I didn't have to write one each time.

Yours truly,
Mrs. White

Kevin fall down Saturday and had a big lump on his head, it was still there Monday, so I tooke him to the hospital. It is a very miner thing, but I wanted to have it check.

Mrs. Xavier

William will be absent tomorrow due to the funeralization of his cousin.

Mrs. Young

I'm sorry I didn't send the note. I forgot. Brenda vomited on the way to school the last time she was absent.

Thanks
Mrs. Zeller

Angela was absent Thursday because she had a doctors appointment. She was absent Friday because she was ill. If she goes outside would you ask her to put her hat over her ears?

Thank you,
Mrs. Allen

Bobby have had plait in his ears. An have ben runing an hight fever. He had to go to see the Doctor.

Mrs. Blake

Please amitt Leroy to class. I have been in the hospital. So when I came out yesurday, I did have no one to watch me, so Leroy had to stay out of school.

Thank you,
Mrs. Carter

Nancy was absent last week due to a sprain foot. Please excuse her from running or jumping exercises this week.

Thank you,
Mrs. Davis

Yvette was absent yesterday due to illness. She has one Tylenol and a cough drop to take at snack time.
>
> Thank you,
> Mrs. Ellis

Billy has been very sick since Friday with a cold and a bad cough he still has his cough so if you dont mine dont let him run around or get excited because he will get to coughing and then start choking.
>
> Thank you
> Mrs. Franklin

Brian was out of school last Thursday to go to the doctor for his check up. Friday he was sick and Monday we did over sleep.
>
> Mrs. Gray

We kept Michael home yesterday because of the rain. He is going into the hospital next month to have his throat examined.
       Mrs. Hawkins

    Regina has the amas, and she has trouble with her heart. I told her to tell you, but she didn't. Please let her be careful on some of the G.Y.N. exercisers please.
        Mrs. Insley

Please excuse Larry Feb. 5th. He had a high fever with his cold. And he wasn't feeling very well.
       Thank you,
       Mrs. Jefferson

Please excuse Albert from school Dec. 17th through 20th. He was very sick with the flue!
                      Thank you,
                      His Mother

Please excuse Randy from school yesterday as I needed to keep him at home.
                      Thank you,
                      Mrs. Lewis

Betty do not fill to good yesterday.
                      Mrs. Moore

Michelle were not at school yesterday, because we was out of town.

Mrs. Nelson

Please excuse John for being absent from school because he was sick and there were things that we had to tend to before leaving on leave. We had no one to babysit him when he got home from school. He also was running a fever and has a cold.

Thank you,
Mrs. Oliver

Rita stayed home to help me.

Mrs. Payne

Steven will not be at school tomorrow. My babysitter has to work the poles so he won't have anyone to take him off the school bus.

        Mrs. Quigley

    The reason why Ontwon wasn't in school Friday was because we had to go home for a while and see his grandparents and Monday morning he was sick, he had caught a cold when we went home but he is fine now.

            Mrs. Rogers

I kept Andrea home yesterday because of the Valentine program.

        Thank you,
        Mrs. Scott

Please excuse Mary last week for not being in school for she had to be taken to the Doctor because she had a absese ear, so please do not let her join in any outside activities.

Thank you,
Mrs. Thomas

Please excuse Tony for being absent yesterday, he had a bad cough and runee nose.

Mrs. Upjohn

Terry was absent yesterday because I had to take her to the doctor. Please be patient with her because she can not hear. Her ears are infected and backed up with fluid. So if she seems unattentive it's only because you have to speak louder to her.

Thank you,
Mrs. Vaughan

Beverly went to her doctor last Friday. She has alot of pus of her Kidneys and she's on medication. Could you make sure she takes her pill at 12:00 today and every day this week. She has infetigo on her face but I'm putting medicine on her face too for that!
>Thank you kindly,
>Mrs. Waters

Donna went to the doctor yesterday regarding her stomach. She has an enlarged colon resulting from small stools. The pain should be gone hopefully by next week.
>Thank you,
>Mrs. Yates

Arthur ben sick with a cold.
>Think you,
>Mrs. Zimmerman

Mary went to a vabtizim and we came back 3:00.

                         R. Adams

    Please excuse Tommy from school, Monday, Tuesday, and Wednesday. We was having some problems at home that just has to be work out.

                         Thank-You,
                         Mrs. Brooks

Carrie was sick yesterday with her cold.

                         Ms. Clark

Please excuse Emily absent out school. She was out because her period was on. Please except her in.
Thank You
Mrs. Drake

We had to go to North Carolina on something important. Please excuse Betty. Send Betty's work home with her and I will catcher up.
Thank You
Mrs. Edwards

We are sorry Donna was out of school, we had to go out of town on an Emergence! and we diden have no one to keep her so we had to take her with us! Thank you!
Mrs. Ferrell

Tim was out of school because of his tooth. One of them had set up infection, so the dentist couldn't find it until Wed. It is still hurting him some.

Thank You,
Mr. Green

Tina came home from school yesterday upset because you had told her that *you thought* she was too young to wear a bra.

Well, what you think about which under clothes she should or should'nt wear, you can keep to yourself.

Your'e not paid to give your appenion in these matters.

If I think Tina is old enough to wear a bra—then it should'nt matter to anyone else.

I'd like to know at what age you think a girl should begin wearing a bra? Tina is 8 yrs. old.

Mr. Hayes

Peter had to stay home to help me. I am sick with a Bad Cold.

       Mrs. Ivey

  Charles was absent on Tuesday due to prostrationitis.

       Mrs. James

Please excuse Marie for being absent yesterday. I kept her home for a personal reason.

       Thank You,
       Mrs. King

Please excuse Carol's lateness to school this morning. We have had a combination of alarm clock and car problems that made us all late today. We will try not to let it happen again.

Sincerely yours,
Mrs. Lyons

Please excuse Ginny's absence on yesterday. I kept her home.

Mrs. McDonald

I'm sorry Sherry missed school yesterday. She walks to the bus stop with Terry and there was a little trouble with Terry getting ready for school yesterday morning. I let Sherry wait a little to long and she missed the bus, Fred couldn't drive them to school because our car isn't running right.

Sincerely,
Mrs. Newman

Yesterday, Shirley bus was apparently early. She missed the bus. I was told they had a substitute driver. Please excuse her absence.

Mrs. O'Hara

Theodore was out yesterday with a muscular spasm (charlie horse) in his neck.

Mrs. Peters

Please excuse Diana for yesterday the 15th. Diana, went to see her doctor yesterday and he told me she has a lot of conjestion in her chest so she's on medication. Please make sure she takes her two pills at Lunch time. Don't allow Diana to run too much cause she gets hot and starts coughing.

Thank you,
Mrs. Quinn

Could you see if Glenda could charge her lunch this week. I will send the money Monday. Please go with her to the office so that lady in there don't have anything smart to say to her. Because the last time I ask her she smarted off to me about it. And she all ways gets her money when I say she will!!

Thank you
Mrs. Ryan

Walter stayed home from school yesterday because I was ill. He helped me around the house.

Mrs. Sawyer

Barbara started the day yesterday by throwing up . . . for the third time in two weeks. The doctor suspects it was caused by allergy drippage. We wish you a Happy and Healthy New Year.

Sincerely,
Mrs. Utz

I am dissappointed in Brenda report card, she never made D and C, every since she been in Sp. class she made A and B and few C. I want her to be put in another class so she wont be with Lucy Ann. I know she can do better than this. I want you to do this for me. I want you to have her class change. Called me today or called this morning.

Mrs. Tucker

If you want the boys, the twins Willie or William to have something clothes, shoes or what ever, and Im not getting them fast enough for you, you get them.

Because really I dont think you or anyone else there at school has the right to tell me when to buy them something.

This has nothing to do with their learning nothing. I asked them before to tell you if you were going to send me a message and it didn't pretain to school, I didn't want to hear it, now Im telling you. When I feel they are able to do more looking after themselves then I will get them the necessary things, until then I have had it.

I can put on brand new under clothes today, and tonight they are tore to threads, if you want William to have shoes, buy them and when they are here if I want them to have onions they will have them.

I have enough problems home. I dont need you to give me more. Send the boys home work home. This I will help with, if I forget to send it the next day then I will send it the following day. A lot of time you want to be able to get me. It not because Im not home its just that I don't answer the phone because Im in the yard or just forget to put the phone in the socket. Dont send any more messages unless its pretaining to school, or their health.

Mrs. Vick

[*A response to a request for the school to administer an auditory screening test to a kindergarten student*]

In light of the fact that, when Jennifer had her school physical in August, her hearing was tested at that time, and, further, within the last year has received a total evaluation at a child development clinic—in which she was evaluated in all areas, not only speech and hearing, but also manual dexterity, I.Q., spacial relations of forms, colours, eyesight, etc., and that these tests all were satisfactory, I consider further testing at this time not only unnecessary but somewhat undesirable. I do not think a child should be feeling that she is under constant surveillance for some sort of vague abnormality: this leads to paranoia and social stereotyping—what I refer to as the "T.V. standard image."

Should Jennifer evidence an inability to comprehend or participate in class, perhaps we can discuss this matter further. In the meantime, I feel that she is a bright child, who can easily grasp the lessons which are presented to her in a kindergarten class. I think kindergarten should help to develop an appreciation for a certain structured learning environment, respect and joy in the learning process itself, and an ability to get along with peers, as well as manners in social situations being reinforced. I do not think that you will find Jennifer lacking in these basic abilities.

Thanking you for your cooperation and concern, I remain.

Yours Sincerely,
Ms. Walters

I keep Rhonda home and give her some medicine because, she have a cold.

Mrs. York

Christopher was sick yesterday and we took him to the Dr's for some medicine for his cough and cold, if it all possible please dont let Christopher outside the Dr. said.

Thank you
Mrs. Ziegler

Jeffery had an ear ach, an he had to go to the Docter's, Firday.

Mrs. Ayres

Rose has had the flu since last friday but she seems to be over it, but feels kind of weak yet. Dont let her run and get too hot. Please!

Thank you
Mrs. Becker